Paper Bells

Phan Nhiên Hạo

Translated by Hai-Dang Phan

The Song Cave

The Song Cave

www.the-song-cave.com

Poems © Phan Nhiên Hạo, 2020

Translations and Preface © Hai-Dang Phan, 2020

Cover image: *Việt Nam: Untitled, Ho Chi Minh City*, 1995 © An-My Lê

Design and layout by Janet Evans-Scanlon

ISBN: 978-1-7340351-2-4
Library of Congress Control Number: 2020932217

FIRST EDITION

Contents

Preface

Phan Nhiên Hạo was born in 1967 in Kon Tum, in the Central Highlands of Vietnam, a mountainous area close to the border with Laos and Cambodia. His father was an officer in the South Vietnamese Army and his mother was a housewife, the family living at times on the military base and at others in town. Literature was part of his family culture, their house was filled with books and literary magazines, his father wrote poetry though never published, and he remembers from an early age how much he enjoyed reading. He began his primary education at a Catholic school for two years, then attended public school. With two cinemas, both close to his house in Kon Tum, he went to see many movies.

In spring 1975, everything changed. Kon Tum province saw heavy fighting during the war, and in March of 1975, when the North Vietnamese Army launched its decisive military campaign throughout the South, Phan was evacuated with his mother and two younger brothers on a military cargo plane to Đà Nẵng, his father's hometown. The family eventually relocated to Phan Thiết, where his mother's extended family stayed, and where Phan spent many subsequent years growing up. During the strategic retreat from the highlands in March, his father perished. Saigon fell on April 30, 1975, and seven-year old Phan found himself on the losing side of the war. His father's body was never found, and his death in and of itself made a profound mark on the poet. "I had nothing to do with the war, but the war had everything to do with me," Phan Nhiên Hạo writes in an unusually personal essay called "This Year I Am The Same Age As My Father."

In the late '70s through the early '90s, life in reunified Vietnam became especially difficult if not unbearable for individuals and families associated with the military and government of the former Republic of South Vietnam, and roughly two million people fled the country by any possible means between 1975 and 1995. Escaping a country requires precious time, money, and connections, none of which Phan Nhiên Hạo's mother or extended family possessed. To overcome the political difficulties of his family background, Phan Nhiên Hạo strove to become one of the best literature students in the country, and he succeeded, winning national scholarships and student prizes. In the summertime, he often stayed in the countryside with his uncles on his father's side. They had managed to keep a private library of over one hundred books, including banned books by writers from South Vietnam before 1975 and foreign writers from the West deemed ideologically suspect. Over a few summers, Phan read them all.

Phan Nhiên Hạo moved to Saigon, now officially renamed after Hồ Chí Minh. His hard work had paid off; he gained entrance to the Teacher's College, devoting himself to his education and avoiding military service that would have likely sent him to occupied Cambodia. He majored in literature, reading the assigned Soviet literature but ignoring his teachers' Socialist analyses, and he began composing his own poems. As a young poet he read French, German, and Russian literature in translation, and was drawn particularly to the French Existentialists whose philosophy of the absurd helped him combat the hardships in his own life. His first publications were inward, melancholic, and slightly elevated poems in local newspapers (see "Day Flowers in the Highlands" and "May"). He made a name for himself in literary circles in Saigon, and hung out with the iconclastic poet Nguyễn Quốc Chánh, the unacknowledged trailblazer of post-1975 Vietnamese poetry. But Phan Nhiên Hạo's life and career as a published poet, at least in Vietnam, was short-lived.

In 1991, Phan left Vietnam through the Orderly Departure Program, a legal emigration program that established a safer means of exodus for those, particularly individuals and families associated with the South Vietnamese military, wishing to leave. On departure day, he did not feel safe until the plane was in the air, the country fading from sight.

————

At twenty-four, Phan Nhiên Hạo arrived in the United States, young enough to start over in crucial ways, but old enough to carry in himself the cargo of his Vietnamese identity, history, and language; and his initial years here followed the restless itinerary of the new immigrant. Atlanta was the first city where he found a job, but it was not the place to put down roots. He rode by Greyhound bus from Atlanta to Seattle, a cross-country road trip whose passage and passengers he commemorates in the poem "Greyhound, 1992." In Seattle, where he lived for two and half years, he took classes at a community college in the morning and worked various odd jobs in the afternoons and evenings, including as a newspaper delivery man and janitor. He preferred cleaning large office spaces at night; it was quiet, nobody was around, and there was time to think. (See "Nights Working as a Janitor in Seattle.") After Seattle, he moved to Los Angeles. In Southern California, he was close to Little Saigon in Orange County and became part of the largest population of Vietnamese outside of Vietnam. For his poetry, and in his life, this meant continued contact with Vietnamese native speakers and émigré writers.

Determined to continue his studies, Phan Nhiên Hạo pursued a B.A. at UCLA, majoring in American Literature and Culture, and would also earn a Master's in Library Science there. He immersed himself in the study of American writers, and later translated the work of American poets—Wallace Stevens, William Carlos Williams, Frank O'Hara, and Charles Simic—into Vietnamese. At UCLA, Phan Nhiên Hạo found African American literature particularly instructive and inspiring as a poet still grappling with past and present injustices. Literature, he saw, could be an act of social justice that demanded a reckoning with one's history. "I became more confident in my own voice and proud of who I am," Phan has said. This encounter may have partly contributed to the greater directness and social awareness of his poetry. Another influence would have been the continued neglect and suppression of alternative voices and histories in the Vietnamese diaspora, which were (and continue to be) unpublished—and unpublishable—by the state-run presses in Vietnam and unassimilable to mainstream American literary tastes.

Phan Nhiên Hạo's first collection, *Thiên Đường Chuông Giấy* (*Paradise of Paper Bells*, 1996), written mostly during those first five years in the United States, introduced to Vietnamese-language readers the work of a younger, post-war generation writer whose poetry was a mix of native and foreign influences and the product of his own imagination. Registering the aftershocks of displacement and the bewilderment of existing in a new adopted homeland, his poems captured the everyday surreality of being a Vietnamese immigrant in the United States during the '90s. Many defining features of his poetry were already present early on: the homespun resourcefulness of means; the swerves of the surreal within the real; the deceptively simple language and plain-spoken voice; the commitment to a South Vietnamese refugee memory and the floating life of an exile poet; the quiet defiance and endurance. The poems tended to be short, elliptical, and imagistic, the lyric dispatches of a Vietnamese exile poet on a strange shore. Phan published his poems then and after in the leading overseas Vietnamese literary journals in print and online, like the California-based *Hợp Lưu*, Sydney-based *Tiền Vệ* and Berlin-based *Talawas*—these names may mean nothing to Anglophone readers, but to Vietnamese-language writers and readers they represented what was most vital in contemporary Vietnamese literature.

His following collection, *Chế Tạo Thơ Ca 99-04* (*Manufacturing Poetry 99-04*), published in 2004, showed a poet willing to write more outwardly, more boldly and dangerously, taking not only thematic risks, but formal ones. Phan here experiments with collage techniques and longer forms, while sharpening the speed and attack of shorter poems. Many of the poems address specific historical events, cultural myths and symbols, and are often pierced with laughter, sarcasm, and disgust. The dissident politics of Phan Nhiên Hạo's poetry resound precisely at a historical moment when the United States and Vietnam are reestablishing diplomatic and economic relations, and in the cultural and literary sphere much of the talk is about peace and reconciliation. Refusing to get with the political program, Phan Nhiên Hạo's was a recalcitrant voice that was neither conciliatory nor nostalgic. Instead, Phan's poems told the open secrets of Vietnam's postwar record of Communist excess and corruption, reeducation camps, refugee exodus, and cultural amnesia, while giving voice to the unsung lives of Vietnamese in the diaspora in poems like "Meeting a Cab Driver in New York" and "Seattle Memory."

15 years passed before the publication, in spring 2019, of Phan Nhiên Hạo's third and most recent poetry collection, *Summer Radio*. In those years, he moved to northern Illinois to work as a research librarian specializing in Southeast Asia; he and his wife raised two children; he earned a second advanced degree, a Masters in Cultural Anthropology; he traveled internationally for academic conferences and for work; he became a frequent contributor as a critic to the leading Vietnamese literature and culture magazines online, unafraid to offer controversial opinions, and also started his own online magazine for a brief period; and he continued to write his own poems, though they appeared at greater intervals. *Summer Radio* finds the poet leading an increasingly reflective life, with one foot in the present and one in the past. There is a more relaxed, retrospective cast to the collection, which opens with four previously uncollected poems written during his student days in Vietnam. Chronic sorrow and loneliness are increasingly complicated by an insurgent anger and dark humor, evident especially in the acerbic portrayals of contemporary Vietnam. The poems return to Vietnam, not just through memory as in earlier books, but now through Phan's travels

back to his native land, and they return as well to refugee memories of the poet's early years in the United States. There is also a renewed restlessness, with the poet mapping an expanded geography of imagination, an altogether elsewhere.

The two enduring themes of Phan Nhiên Hạo's poetry remain: his American life as a Vietnamese refugee and exiled poet, and his commitment to a more just memory and history for South Vietnamese. Cultivating a scrupulous solitude, Phan expresses a world-weariness, existential exhaustion, and depletion of resources as a poet in exile. Yet he summons the strength to remember, just as he calls upon the strength to forget—long enough to sit down and write, with whatever materials and methods are near at hand, or as he puts it in "Manufacturing Poetry":

> On an afternoon with nothing to do
> I sit manufacturing poems
> out of sixteen screws, two metal plates,
> and four wheels. Poems fueled
> by a mix of strife, hope, love, and futility.

Echoing the longer title of his first collection, I have chosen *Paper Bells* to name the present gathering of poems because it rings with the muted music of this poet's voice of solitude. Neither a "best of" nor a "representative" selection, *Paper Bells* is something more personal, practical, and fortuitous. The collection is arranged chronologically, beginning with a small clutch of three poems from 1989 and 1990 when the poet lived in Vietnam, and then sampling headlong from his three collections in Vietnamese published after he immigrated to the United States. The book excludes poems from Phan Nhiên Hạo's first two collections that have already been translated into English by Linh Dinh and published in the single volume, *Night, Fish, and Charlie Parker* (Tupelo Press, 2005). The majority of the poems here, about the last two thirds of the selection, were written after 2004 and were subsequently published in the 2019 collection, *Summer Radio*. Around half of these poems were translated in collaboration, with Phan Nhiên Hạo knocking out rough transliterations that I could work on slowly and freely with a good dictionary, e-mails back and forth with him when necessary, occasional consultations with my parents (I had my mother read out loud a few of the poems so I could better hear and understand them), and always my own poet's emergency kit.

These poems represent the result of over ten years of literary collaboration and friendship. There was little design, but much desire in the process. I first began translating Phan Nhiên Hạo's poems when I was a graduate student working somewhat aimlessly on a dissertation about literature as reconciliation after the Vietnam War. Years later, often when my own poetry was going nowhere, I continued to read and translate his poems, and in this way, they helped keep the possibility of poetry alive. My Vietnamese is neither a foreign nor a native tongue, but an uncanny one, at once my most intimate and my most estranged language. I did not learn Vietnamese formally until I was in my late twenties, and disused as an everyday language it atrophies quickly. While I was born in Vietnam, I arrived in the United States at the age of two and grew up in Wisconsin speaking English, though my parents speaking Vietnamese would always be the sound of home. The experience of translating these poems by Phan Nhiên Hạo has been something like the experience of flying home, and in flight I am continually reminded that we are accidents of history and geography.

For the past thirty years, the poet Phan Nhiên Hạo has been living and writing in exile with no regrets, off-center, in the shadows of no man's land, mostly invisible and unknown, undomesticated, and free. I will be his translator and collaborator—and his witness.

Hai-Dang Phan
Iowa City, Iowa

Rainy Day Song

It rains morning to night
I still have enough money to last until tomorrow
so I'll just lie down and cry
for this joy and that pain
from those moldy days
without sunlight to shine on the lies
or moon to illuminate the money
gold-plating dreams
when sadness was the flipside of hunger

It rains morning to night
I still have enough to survive a hundred more years
so I'll just lie down and sing
man's forever song
about the infinite horizon
vast enough for countless cemeteries
don't stress
we have a million lives

It rains morning to night
rivers rise, oceans bloat, fields give birth
to thousands of frogs
heaven and earth cry out
for the silence
for the rice to stand erect
for you to harvest the crop
and feed the birds with leftover seeds

It rains morning to night
I have just enough for a haircut
to buy a bar of soap
to wash the streets
so I can walk on the immaculate pavements
inspect the parade of houses
passing solemnly as time puffs out
its bronzed chest
pinned with medals
each one for a day I lived
in the pits of pain.

(1989)

Day Flowers in the Highlands

Hibiscus by the fence under the morning sky
a rooster crowing at midday
last night the sound of sadness
stepping barefoot
into the house on stilts by the stream
I listen to your voice in the final moments
vibrating a farewell without promise of reunification
the moon drowns in fog
and I drift
time drifts
to the country of unspoken things
where the yellow flowers
bloom for those who journey far away
your eyeliner smeared
writing love on the hills and rocks
the monsoon has begun
our time is up to stay longer
inside each other
we'll miss our walk through the fertile valley
now we're just a man and woman waving to each other
torn
every which way
what's the use of broken petals?
I ask you, day flowers on the mountaintop

(1990)

May

May
impatient birds melt their wings under the sun
a wildfire attempts to escape from its own ashes

May
the rain returns to the city and forgets its way
lightning flickers cloud to cloud
reluctant to strike
you kneel behind the departed
praying for distant winds
to bring back the listless clouds
delay all passersby
keys clinking hands fumble
to open their lives

May
the bus kicks up red dust
carrying away the homesick

(1990)

Seattle Memory

Day rains, stops, afternoon blazes and night comes late. Summer in Seattle, I remember Da Lat. The little afternoons tucked away into a corner of that city, where I crossed hills, sun shining like red fruit ripening, tranquil lakes. Penniless one morning I went down into the city, over footpaths of fallen petals. I lived there. Days graceful and carefree, days flickering between dream and reality. I didn't question myself. I dozed in a wooden box that smelled of pine, and dreamt. It was my spot for dreaming. People were planting cabbage and flowers, hungry and poor. A dream. Disaster was coming. I sat on distant chairs, walked beneath sheets of rain and asked the grass on the hilltop why it grows. As a snake slithered by, I heard dinosaurs roar and volcanoes erupt. I lived in my own private bubble.

Now I live in this city, with its outdoor markets, soaring freeways, days of heat, nights of fog, mornings of snow. How far is Da Lat? The blue ocean lies between. Nobody left for me to miss, I have little to say. The world is vast, see yourself spinning. Ahead, the road joins earth to heaven. Summer days in the North are very long. My sleep, disturbed. I drive on slippery roads. My writing, haphazard. I try to stay calm at all costs. Even so, I work hard. I'm a miner inside a cave that has collapsed, everyone escaped. Not a soul knows I've survived. From ages ago.

(1993)

Wearing a Red Shirt in the Afternoon

Wearing a red shirt
I dream a bloody dream
as the afternoon goes into labor
and the sun shoots flames at human patience
With claws and fur
I stride into the coliseum
waving my arms, charging forward, then collapsing
oh flag flying up high
witness to the bridge jumpers
the losers and heartbroken chain-smokers
never stoop to sympathize

In the glass living room
in my red shirt I look outside aimless
dreaming of becoming an immortal bullfighter
only to realize I'm that puppy
struck down by a car

(1994)

No Rain Today

No rain today
this afternoon a bird fell out of the sky
the world seems to change
yesterday's little girl is now a woman
sometimes the young man feels ancient
occasionally things can be washed clean in the rain
sometimes your methods betray you
thunder frightens the child
and he starts to hate the rain

The tropical roads are choked with decayed leaves
people are too lazy to smile in the poor city
others are cheating on the train running toward nothingness
this morning when my car overheated
I was afraid of missing my train
even though I'm a ticketless passenger
duped by machines
and tired
the world doesn't change after all
there are always crowds cheering when you fall
the only things I know are
this bird is dead
and there's no rain.

(1996)

The Definition of Summer

These days I get to live inside the very definition of summer
blue skies, AC, water melons, and ice cream
my credit cards are almost maxed out
my fourteen dollar per hour day job
is tedious but temporary
weekends I'm at the library
looking left, looking right, hunched over
my English and Vietnamese, my assimilation and return
you won't find a better immigrant than this one

On the road to Vegas
at night the moon
rises like the curved cup of the bra
I wear on my face
driving through the desert with one eye
tomorrow morning
I'll play slots
gamble until there's nothing left to lose
then summer will be perfect.

(1997)

8

Saturday, May 10, 1998

Saturday morning, May 10, 1998
nothing special really
the birthday of thousands of people not me
nothing special really
some whales wash ashore dead
I open a can of sardines
fish without heads think in silence
I open my hand
the lines on my palm tell me it's not time to die yet
I open Walt Whitman
leaves of grass still lush in the middle of a haughty smile
I spread your legs wide open
a sad creature is born
I open the door of morning
it's already past 10
Saturday morning nothing special really
except I am short of 25 cents
for laundry

(1998)

Paper Bells

The paper bells hanging from the ceiling
make no sound.
Summer has begun.
I stand naked in the afternoon
in the middle of the yard watching my shadow
flowing like ink from my feet
a piece of night.
A one-story house holding 60,000 gallons of gasoline.
My head is a flame
throwing open the door
to each blaze.
My spirit can't take flight.
The paper bells make no sound.

(1998)

The Copper Plated Street Car

The copper plated streetcar
runs on sunlight and emits ocean sounds
In San Francisco pigeons often lie dead on the tracks
This morning I left the tiny room you once compared to a prison cell
where every night I torture myself by forty-seven TV channels.

You worry I think you're too young
You say, "Don't try too hard, you can stay home on rainy days"
I bring you this gold fish in a wine glass
observe and ponder the question of freedom
recall Nelson Mandela and the movements he spawned

I think a decent man like him must have thought much about women
while in prison
even once in a while resorting to jerking off
Such matters are natural and have nothing to do with respect
We're all prisoners of some sort

We've entered a new century only a few centimeters from the old
and I'm only a glance away from my fellow passengers.
It's impossible to stop the noise from their endless arguments
about the dead pigeons, IT applications, and the meaning of next
month's summer parade.

I ride the copper plated streetcar through streets named after the dead
through intersections tired of smelling like armpits
toward the beach
where the sand crabs race against their own shadows.

(2001)

Don't Die Another Person's Death

Now onto the task
of dying another person's death.
Nations, peoples, their suppressions—
I can only die my own death.
Never say, "I will die for . . ."

Outlast the quiet afternoons,
the nights lighting matches looking for my slippers
while the stars fall on my face.
How to live another person's life
as if your soul dwelled in another body.
Never say, "I live for . . ."

Gossips are like ocean waves
forming on the horizon, louder when closer,
crashing on the rocks, humiliated.
Language always comes
from the roof of my mouth, my red tongue, my private anger.
Never say, "On behalf of . . ."

When I arrive, another person has just left,
someone else will be coming, others are always waiting.
They wear traditional *ao dai*, suits bought from flea markets,
some wear Postmodern hats, holding bottles of green medicine oil
to soothe history's four-thousand-year stomach ache.

We all line up outside a restroom—
even in this business I must bring my own paper.

(2003)

E-mail from Nguyen Quoc Chanh

Been in Da Lat
a week already
Saigon was too hot
hotter than years past
I am more afraid of people every day
even the grass and trees looked a little fried.

Rained here yesterday
black clouds filled the sky
and flies coated the ground
inside a pho joint I asked someone
what's up with all the flies
he said it's fly season.

Cheers.

(2003)

Greyhound, 1992

In '92 I crossed the country
from Atlanta to Seattle by bus.
I had $300 and about that much English.
Over the flat fields of the Midwest
I saw cows crowded like ants.
The air smelled like shit for miles upon miles.
The locals seemed unfazed.
Had I stayed long enough
I wouldn't smell anything either
I guess.

Many black folks rode the bus.
Only later did I learn this was the easiest way
for the poor to travel state to state.
They have lots of time and little money.
In the restroom of a transfer station in Denver
a white kid offered me a joint and something else.
That was also the first time I saw an Indian
not from a movie. He was too drunk
to remember what tribe he belonged to.
He didn't carry a gun or bow,
but held a tall boy while slumped in a corner.
I turned down the joint and something else to avoid
becoming a yellow man who exists only in the movies.

I sat beside a Hmong dude—shorter than me!
This guy drank milk the whole trip.
You might have thought he was a loser

hoping for a second growth spurt.
But I know why he guzzled so much milk.
It's simple, his stomach hurt.
I, too, suffered from gastritis once.
The result of years of starvation
and bitterness from growing up in a piss-poor nation.
He clutched the jugs (Made in the USA, 75 cents)
like a pair of fake breasts you toss in the trash after sucking.
Back then, I felt like an immigrant made from plastic,
resilient and resistant to all types of acids.

In 1992, the Greyhound from Atlanta to Seattle
only cost $85 for the 2,600 mi. journey.
America, you swallowed me down your throat
cheaper than dirt.

(2004)

1858

The camera pans for a way to film the face
of a mountain. Artificial light launched
from the cannons of warships
anchored in the gulf of Tourane
causes bats to drop from the ceiling of the Palace
and blood to redden the river Huong.

The position of the camera is no accident.
In 1858 it aimed to civilize
our country by the Seventh Art.
146 years later, we're still making
serial porn.

(2004)

Da Lat 1998-2002

Returning to Da Lat in 2002 on the fourth day of the Lunar New Year
I no longer recognized Da Lat.
I saw a beetle trying to flip itself over its legs
tiny pines waving at the sky.
I ran up to Cu Hill but it had turned into a breast
for Taiwanese businessmen to climb on top and squeeze every day.
I went down to the lake,
its right side had dried up, its left side was trashed,
the lakeshore lousy with snack vendors and souvenir photographers.

I stopped by Café Tung, now a hotspot filled with customers of
    all species.
Here was the place, in 1987, in my corduroys, in shoes borrowed
    from my pal Bang
that were too big I had to stuff them with paper,
where I sat smoking cigarettes while waiting for the mediocre
    coffee to drip into my cup.
When you are 20 years old without a future but very sharp teeth,
you can enjoy chewing on your life in Da Lat,
you can stand with serenity under the waterfalls of your suffering
as if standing in the middle of a strawberry field looking at the
    little temple
on a hill on the other side where a guard dog is being raised
to protect the faith, where the old monk died after refusing his
    last meal
so that the novice monk could have a bit of rice.
When the novice monk grew up he became a desperate lover.

Da Lat now has gotten fat,
with streets stretched way out, houses recklessly thrown up.
Motor scooters have all stolen the peace of morning.
Days are full of rough and tumble men from the crap provinces
who maraud the soft bodies of young women,
mug the gentle language, maim the land.
The world is full of pawns shoved by slogans and guns
        to cross rivers.

I drank my bottled water, and I retreated to the Global Trek Hotel
next to the Palace of King Bao Dai. Through the foggy window
        I saw a woman
shouldering two bamboo baskets balanced on a pole.
I don't know what she was carrying—
but I know the weight of life stuck in a valley.

(2004)

Manufacturing Poetry

On an afternoon with nothing to do
I sit manufacturing poems
out of sixteen screws, two metal plates,
and four wheels. Poems fueled
by a mix of strife, hope, love, and futility.
Enough to run from America to China
in a pitch-black tunnel bisecting the Earth's core.

Blasting open fate
I tunnel deep.

(2004)

At Home in the Summer
with a Remote Control

Inside the house during a hot summer in the valley
you can change colors like a chameleon,
from pink romanticism to brown realism,
or a glitzy literary fashion.
In any case you shouldn't eat
the sugarcane
spitted out by the toothless.

I like to watch TV and check in on the world
happening inside the rectangular box,
a fish tank without air bubbles
each thing distant, unspoiled, and odorless—
until the day I find myself
a character in the evening news.
That will be the moment I see clearly
nothing is completely immune
from a remote control.

(2004)

Meeting a Cab Driver in New York

The yellow cab runs on roads ripped open
by earthquakes never sealed
above our heads skyscrapers veer off
Nguyen Van B. has lived in New York for 28 years
he's still not fluent in English
his French is better

Robbed three times at gunpoint,
B. says: "Anything worth losing I've already lost,
country, youth, dreams
Back in Saigon my family had two servants
and one chauffeur
now I'm the chauffeur of millions of people
In this city you catch a cab by whistling
just wave your hand I'll run right up to you
like a yellow dog called Taxi . . .

. . . don't worry, no need to tip me,
we're both Vietnamese, after all."

(2004)

The Poor in Vietnam: A Survey

With an average annual income of $485 per person in 2003
Vietnam ranks as one of the poorest nations in the world.
90% of Vietnam's poor live in the countryside,
with the poorest found in the mountainous North, the Highlands,
and upper Central region.
Most of the urban poor live in slums
underneath bridges or down in the deepest recesses of alleyways
Their lives have become destitute
thanks to joblessness, meager wages, and chronic debt.

The poor lead vulnerable lives
just once falling ill or losing a bet
will flush a life down the can.

Often isolated the poor pay no mind to the outside
They value neighbors just like themselves
engaged in risky business and who go for broke.
(This problem also pertains to those utterly lacking in literary talent.)
The poor belong to the Tradition   of Hunger and Poverty.
They adore legends.

The Vietnamese are skilled martial artists
But generation after generation they get massacred
by their rulers.

Macro level changes could greatly impact the poor
Rulers, know the poor will eventually run out of their own
    blood to sell
they will demand payback   in blood.

(2004)

Illinois, April 25, 2007

The up elevator opens onto a floor full of books
gutter water from a tame rainy season
is just enough to drown grass
growing nostalgically after winter
pine cones roll off the roof
dropping onto the yard caked with unraked leaves
and a bewildered dog watches passing cars in this small town

Clouds sprout
on the smooth face
of a young man carving a wooden figure
a half-naked god
whose stomach is filled
with mistakes and pleasures
like a box full of love letters and coins

Glory to those who live in solitude
and die like eagles on snowy mountaintops
far from senseless people
with clay heads, concrete legs, and tin tongues
who pray nervously
from church benches casting fearful shadows

From the library you can see the lake
a house and a tomb of fish
see the carefree roads
cutting through the harmony of the Plains

Sixty-five miles west of Chicago
the day smells like peanut butter
on the fields of glory tractors are busy drawing
the austere face of freedom.

(2007)

The City of Ant Nests

A child emerges from a canal of black water
wanders selling knock-off hopes
ash mixed into shoe polish
saliva stirred into boiling soup
clouds hung out to dry on electrical lines
desperately entangled.
Using conch shells to communicate   trucks hauling stone
smash on a one-way street.

Dawn ferments in the alley café
submissive like spoiled fish.
Behind glass pizza melts
foreigners   in the age of integration   and boxers
haggle in the backpacker district.

Between the muscles are red tendons
elastic but tightening up
while all the needles have been snapped off
and the sky drips ozone.

Saigon
vice-citizen
stands on one leg
hiccups
on a colorful ant nest.

(2008)

26

Flamenco Vietnamese Opera

Looking at the stone sculpted face I don't hear a thing
only see a row of perfect teeth
a mixed-media exhibit of nylon and banana leaves.

A fortune teller recounts all the times he's faked being blind
foreseeing a century without light.

Time is a perfect crime
convictionless and dissolving
in a solution of weakness and sewage.

At humdrum speeds
the third-world train smells of urine
you always miss something
like the truth passing by outside the window.

My job is not to spy
on God in the shower
an unstable and left-leaning old woman
with too much scar tissue and damaged vital organs
wheezing like a sleeping tortoise
indifferent to humans who buy life insurance.

In the parking lot
there's an enormous bird egg cooked by the sun
—the unfinished work
of the filmmaker who was executed
for daring to make a movie about the great leader,
The Sadist.

The world is full of dry eyes
and corny people trying to flamenco Vietnamese opera
while I'm inside the laundry machine
cradling a sawed-off shotgun.

(2008)

Fish in a Well

When we were young my cousin
caught fish and fried them
some he dropped into the well
its shallow muddy water
he said: "These are the lucky ones"

Everyday
the metal bucket
plunged to the bottom a dozen times
I knew it must be hell
for the survivors

Around that same time my uncle was gasping for air in a
    "reeducation camp."

(2008)

Morning at O'Hare

hot coffee
expandable air
buttery smells
trash aplenty
vague jazz
sentimental notes
airplanes departing
airplanes landing
nothing exciting
crowds escalating
compromises ahead
wordy rainbows
tacky ads
wasted colors
televised history
wasted blood
shitty food
toilets flushing
gurgle gurgle

(2009)

Wash Your Hands

From here inside and outside look all the same to me
this half and that half are evenly pale
winter shoveling snow   a game of flies in the tropics
the swampy city a breeding ground for mosquitoes
where breasts are squeezed in the beer halls until broken
and thrown into the bloody river with hyacinths

Last night I dreamt of the dead picking up cans
not for cash   but to use as incense holders
all along Highway One from the South to the North
Gentlemen, this is no trivial matter,
another story about art for art's sake, or art for life,
this is the story about a cut the length of decades
about an incestuous history
spawning pig-humans who buried people alive.

Sometimes I push the door open onto the future
but the counterfeit past snuffs out the present
I say   open open   flush flush
to all of us eating where we shit
let's put down our bowls and take a walk instead
the young, the old, and the well-fed
there's still time, if only a few moments
to wash your hands before escorting your souls
embarking for the afterlife
baggage and all.

(2009)

A Travel Guide for Hue

Thua Hien Province, as often noted in history books, has many
    sea mouths.
There is Thuan An, which boasts a temple for worshipping whales,
a royal travel station, and affluent villages,
once called the City of Thuan An by the French.
There is also the sea mouth at Tu Hien,
whose deadly waves devoured countless boats.
Angry King Ly Than Tong ordered his soldiers
to fire two cannonballs into the waves.
One wave was fatally wounded, turning water into blood.
One wave fled to the high seas, desperate.
From then on the village boats traveled in peace.

Later King Tu Duc also ordered
to fire the cannons directly upon French's war ships.
One wave was fatally wounded, turning water into blood.
One wave fled to the high seas, desperate.
From then on French ships came and went as they pleased.

Dear tourists, please note that King Tu Duc was a poet.

(2009)

Nights Working as a Janitor in Seattle

There are times in your life
attacked by vacuum cleaners and rags
you flee one floor to the next
all night, a lost soldier
from a throng of defeated immigrants.

Peering into countless toilets each day
by the end they become mere loudspeakers to you
babbling foul songs
about desperation and hope.

Your duty is
to disinfect the underside of life
disappear all the evidence before sunrise.

You drive home through clouds of steam
rising from street grates and manholes like coffee for the waking city
on your right is the ocean
a white ship sinking
nobody notices.

(2011)

A Guitarist in Exile

This guitarist stretches his strings
from one time zone to another,
from the silt beds of the Mekong River
to the fields of the Midwest.
The sky where he now lives is often cloudy,
the cows slaughter-ready.

His songs are about love,
the smell of a road after a tropical storm.
He sings of exile, blizzards,
and empty parking lots.
His past is like a street musician
faking blindness. His present
is like a hot air balloon
aloft and waiting to fall back to the earth.
His future is just a TV
in a nursing home losing its signal.

He has nothing but music
in this hard-of-hearing world.
And this makes him feel as useless
as those times during Sunday blackouts
he would lie in a tiny room
on Nguyen Tri Phuong Street naked
and fanning himself
in Saigon during the 1980s.

(2011)

March in Atlanta

I can't recall the color of that March
but the snow was melting the same day in Chicago.
I flew south to Atlanta,
walked around a sparkling downtown
circled by dismal districts.

Setting out
I explored the monotony of manhole covers
and observed the immature flies of spring
vibrating nervously atop pathetic flower pots
in front of a liquor store dotted with cigarette butts.

Incidents took place,
but I was far from any bloody scenes.
I bought a map to make it clear
you are here, an outsider.

In the Coca-Cola Museum
I pissed more than I drank
of the different sodas
tricking my thirst.

I heard America burp.

(2011)

At Zero Meridian

Not enough time to search
before I myself become lost
among the faded letters
on a carbon copy
caught in an extinct typewriter.

No more inspiration left for discoveries
before I too become a mystery
missing on a boat where there's no water
the country has a long coast but few islands
no help whatsoever for the exile

No more afternoons spent there
the days a hot mess, mouths filled with dust
population exhausted, traffic jammed, city crushed
memory often scrambles the colors
I need a new pair of sunglasses

"You shouldn't swallow watermelon seeds
because the vine might sprout from your mouth"
advised a middle-aged man over the phone
on the beach wearing pants
in summertime.
"Don't worry," I said, "Nothing can grow
on a life that has lost its ground."

(2011)

Flying a Single Engine Airplane,
Fuel Almost Empty, and Needing to Pee

How much longer can I keep flying
this arthritic airplane
looking down at the line of people
waiting for some meat at the Temple of Literature.

In this airspace I'm handsome
with a scarf used to staunch the bleeding,
and a pair of brown shoes about to be divorced.

Solitude   demands ample fuel
but there's no help from the ground.
A municipal airport   in a third-world country,
the geriatric and illiterate air traffic controller
dozes off next to a broken
vending machine.

The altimeter gets confused
between the gecko and its shadow.
Impossible to land safely,
but no more dangerous than this.
The only question left for me
is to pee or not to pee
inside the cockpit.

(2011)

After the Storm

A film was projected on the tattered curtains of clouds:

an elephant with sawed-off tusks
trunk reaching for the sun

leaping over a rainbow
a horse lands on the endless horizon

above a suspect village
a bird zips from one lightning rod to the next

summer afternoon, an airplane drags itself across the sky
like a voice-over in an old movie

growling.

(2011)

Fragments

Toothless day, ghost gray wind
for hours I photograph my thoughts
then develop them into spotty pics.

Kids are anonymous
even if their names are "Innocence" and "Happiness."

The atmosphere in the public restroom
is very earnest
because the buzzing flies.

A rusty gun is still capable of killing someone,
but a feeble mind can't do shit.

The bridge is long
the sky is pale
he   walks   while   pissing
onto the creatures breathing through gills.

South of Cape Ca Mau
the islets break free from their anchor lines to float into the gulf
fleeing the ass kissers.

If you can fly out of yourself
you will become an extraordinary astronaut.

For each of his own prayers
God has to listen to ten from his enemy.
No problem though, God's hearing aid was broken long ago.

He wants to smell fragments of the world before sitting down to eat
but his nose keeps bleeding.
From an old turntable Louis Armstrong gravely rasps:
"What a wonderful World."

(2011)

Instructions for Writing

Write sharply like a nail driven into a plank.
Write swiftly like wind blowing through a village plague.
Write quietly like coals burning inside the earth.
Write fiercely like a wounded lion on the brink of death.
Write cautiously like a train plowing through a foggy morning.
Write sensitively like a dragonfly before a storm.
Write pleasure all over the sand, then connect the dots.
Write sorrow on the water, let the waves do the carrying.
Write solitude onto a lantern, keeping vigil until the light burns out.
It's possible to write briefly, but don't skip verbs,
stagnancy will sink punctuation marks.
Write after dusk but not at dawn—
that's when the ghosts return
after collecting more spirit money.
Write prolifically when drunk, though once sober, throw it all
        into the river,
and try not to brag about your intoxications.
Write for the dead, but don't invite the funeral band
because synthetic music suffocates the corpse.
It's fine to write aimlessly, but don't be careless.
Keep language in its solid state with a high melting point.
Write far below zero, like a winter day in Oymyakon.
Write sweating bullets, like summertime in Dallol.
Write in the style of the New York School or Prairie, both are cool,
but don't dance around with a stick
thinking no one can see you.
Write hopelessly like waiting for the moon to fall on the roof and
        break into pieces.

Write hopefully like when I waited for my wife to give birth
  at Tu Du Hospital.
Write unforgettably like in Bangkok six years ago when I saw
a beautiful woman with twelve fingers.
Write mysteriously like all the long nights of my youth
listening to the symphony of the street merchants crying out.
Write handsomely, but pay no attention to symmetry.
Write gorgeously, but avoid cheap face powder.
Write in the middle of a crowd while standing alone,
a "Do Not Disturb" sign around your neck.
When the nameless are executed in the city's square,
write their faces in blood, and never wash your hands—
not until freedom spreads like soap bubbles
from scrubbing history's shameful spots.

(2011)

This Country

This country never had any dinosaurs,
a long-standing problem.
Is this sea of vegetables really necessary
to resurrect non-existent fossils?

This country is being watched by a naked army,
revolutionary leftovers
led by a great monkey
who trained an entire nation to perform circus tricks.

This country is a rainy night
protecting those who stay put but flooding the way home
for those out on patrol
returning wounded and disarmed.

This country was not sufficiently saved,
salty and mushy served on a cracked platter,
owner and chef counting money
in the middle of a backyard filled with empties.

This country crawls left and right
to trenches and underground shelters
no longer a secret but choked and full of eels
escaping from the past.

This country is a rusty bomb
in a recycling plant owned by China,
a deaf explosive
taken apart and sold for scrap.

This country is getting old,
its fields battered patchwork, its rivers fraying threads—
I've taken them off and left for another country
where I keep searching flea markets for something similar.

(2011)

9/11 – Hue Massacre

I listen to the radio commemorating
the day more than three thousand people were evaporated
in New York, New York (Frank Sinatra long gone).

I remember that day
I was in a bar in Saigon filled with cigarette smoke and human meat
marinated in perfume.
(I was an overseas Vietnamese having fun in my home country of the
Viet Cong).
You must have heard of this tropical country.
During the war many lost their lives,
many lost their souls.
There was a massacre in Hue.
About six thousand people were slaughtered
within just a few days during the traditional Tet new year.

The lavish party of devils
has mostly been cleaned up by the victors,
only some saliva remains
and a few faded tombstones
standing among the thorns of memory.

No waterfalls,
            no names,
                        no flowers,
                                    no truths.

These deaths were more useless than fertilizer.

Maybe such a story seems unbelievable
for your analytical mind.
Yet for us, the people who hatched from eggs,
all things are just legends,
including fresh blood.

(2012)

Regarding the Spiritual and Social Situation of Vietnam Today (Observations that are current but abstract and highly general, typical of the deep, sensitive, and brave soul of poets)

Having lost our senses,
we carry on the struggle of cooking maggot corpses
from a busted refrigerator.

Mud dwellers, our goal in life
is to compete for the title
of The Filthiest.

Camped out in the Gentleman's Club chewing dog meat,
the worldly smart asses talk big
then stumble home
to hang themselves upside down
in the style of bats.

Those shady dealmakers,
cunning malignant
clowns (who are rightly
scorned), travel in packs through the slums
plotting land grabs.

Hope is a gas station—
SOLD OUT.
Look at these few sorry daydreamers
pushing their scooters around
so tiresomely.

(2012)

Saigon on a Good Day

Saigon is sunniest at seven, but only becomes honest at midnight. For breakfast everyone has fried eggs, bbq pork ribs, and coffee. It doesn't matter, all meals are the same across the country. Everything is thriving and gorgeous always.

That was 2001, the year I returned to Saigon, back in the gutter. Sometimes in life you fall into a ditch on an idle battlefield where you can't stick your head up, and desertion is not an option. All you can do is sit on a helmet with bullet holes and watch the rats eat the corpses.

I got around on a motor scooter and got paid to churn out copy for an ad agency, the kind of writing that teaches you how to conserve words and twist your brain. The part I hated most was artfully painting over money with a yellow coat of pretension. It was easy money provided you knew how to slick back your hair with soy sauce and your own saliva.

Once on Ngo Thoi Nhiem Street I saw an old woman squatting against one of the high walls of the hospital, weeping, tears pouring out of her face like fresh juice squeezed from a sugar cane machine.

What had caught my attention was her strange way of crying. It was as if she was hiding something, constantly wiping her eyes with a wrinkled old scarf so her tears wouldn't overflow into street and upset anyone eating their breakfast of fried eggs, bbq pork ribs, and coffee. Pulling up to her I politely asked, "Is everything okay, auntie?" She turned her panicked face up and said, "My daughter is lying in the hospital. I'm just waiting for money to be sent from our home in the countryside. Don't worry about me, mister, don't worry."

She tried to appear cheerful so I'd stop with the questions, leave her alone, thinking she wasn't bothering anyone, so she could simply go back to being an pitiful old woman in this great city full of rich tycoons and long-legged models, teeming with brutality and stupidity.

She absolutely did not need my money or to tell her story, she was only concerned about being criticized for daring to cry on such a bright sunny morning at seven, the most beautiful time of day in Saigon.

(2012)

Song of Trees

I can't sleep to forget this box I'm inside.
Nice and quiet I slide open the lid
to witness these ants carrying off the fattest death
each day marching past on the slick floor.

There are skinnier deaths
waiting in prison cells before the firing squad.

Ants march in single file
while prisoners walk the wrong way
into history.

But who get to writes history and the traffic laws?

"No one can build a tree,"
says my nine-year-old daughter
as we're sitting
in the shade of a great oak.

You can build a house
loftier than ambitions.
You can construct a theater
to screen the latest illusion.
You can raise a levee
to prevent greater indignation.
You can assemble a regime
solely out of crooks.

You can establish an asylum
to house a whole a society.
You can even create darkness
with invisible bricks and stones.

But you can't build a tree.

A tree springs from its favorite soil.
A tree sheds its leaves according to seasons.
A tree may bear fruit or choose not to.
A tree will fast when the sun is too violent.
A tree will fall down honorably in the end.

No one can build a tree,
You can't plant a person.

We are freedom's chlorophyll!

(2012)

An Exercise Against Abstraction

Now imagine a child
a small child
wandering the streets of Saigon for a living
in a country where the poor have two choices:
to take a piss in the street
or hold it.

Keep holding that image until your head
cracks
like
a bladder.

And you catch a whiff of your own life
stinking.

(2012)

Summer Radio

Dee dee . . . dum di dee . . .
Good morning brothers and sisters
of broken ear drums.
This is the Voice of Solitude
broadcasting to you live
from America in the middle of a cornfield
on the channel of exile with no regrets.

Today's high temp
will be a hot 98 degree hard-on,
no rain and suffocating atmospheric conditions
due to crazy stories coming from the East.

To rescue her daughter,
a mother set herself on fire.
Two naked women
clasped a body of land.
Trying to save a river
a crowd waved banners across a bridge,
only to be kicked into the water.

Meanwhile, all is quiet in the West.
Business as usual, eat less fat,
drive your car in circles.
Red lights slow disintegration.
Life is an iceberg,
it melts faster on sunny days.

Let's switch to the Reconciliation Program.

Forget all your suffering, humiliation, sorrow and bitterness.

Please call this number to chat,

1 800 382 5968

or

1 800 F U C K Y O U

Dee dee . . . dum di dee . . .

Now for a commercial break . . .

(2012)

Summer in Lisbon

Up in the old castle
he looks out upon the future
and sees himself seated
frozen among the discontent
as the sun sets.

Below lies the old city
with its solemn crumbling facades
he remains a stranger
a guest learning how to use fork and knife
dining at the table of history
littered with leftovers.

He knows time is a tired waiter
who just wants last call for the night.

Still he lingers on his final drink
before settling the bill
standing up and heading back in the dark.

(2017)

Vacation

The airplane passengers disembark
like sperm shooting out of a metal penis.
They carry on their shoulders
colorful backpacks—the nylon DNA
gleaming under tropic sun.
They come to do nothing but sit on the beach
gazing at happiness running around on the sand
declining sex.

A windy day, the black flag
marking a whirlpool
flaps like a dog's thirsty tongue.

(2019)

Vietnamese Horoscopes

Vietnamese are forever young,
until the day they become a spasm
of coughing.
The period in between
we reserve
for bragging.

Are either children
or ready to give up the ghost.
For us there is no so-called "adulthood."
We live ready to be reincarnated
into anybody
not Vietnamese.
Though each day we proudly retell
our origin story—
hatched from one hundred eggs…

The truth is we like omelets
for breakfast
and we've been eating each other
through civil wars.

(2019)

In Berlin

It's already past midnight
but the sun has never been late.
Waiting at the end of the street
the sun will catch a yellow tram and come
meet us in a café just opening its doors.

The yellow trams
of this city are its blood,
running day and night inside a beautiful body
that has passed through pain
through murdering nightmares.

History is a series of seizures.
If lucky we live in the meanwhile,
in periods of peace.
Our task is heavy and hopeless,
trying to cure this madness
while finding food
and searching for happiness
in the yard of our homes like chickens
or up in the trees like crows.

But right now, embracing each other in the dark
bravely and nervously
joyfully and guiltily

we can only make this private history together,
a history that ends with the little death
when you scream the scream of someone decapitated
and fall into the black hole of ecstasy.

(2019)

Acknowledgments

Many thanks to the editors of the following publications, in which these poems, sometimes in earlier versions, first appeared: *Anomalous*, *The Brooklyn Rail*, *Cerise Press*, *diaCRITICS*, *Drunken Boat*, *Mekong Review*, *Music & Literature*, *Sink Review*, *St. Petersburg Review*, *Two Lines Press Online Exclusives*, and *Waxwing*.

"Email to Nguyen Quoc Chanh," "Fish in a Well," "Greyhound, 1992," and "March in Atlanta" were published in *Reenactments* (Sarabande Books, 2019). Thank you, Sarah Gorham and Sarabande Books, for permission to reprint these poems.

I am grateful for a fellowship from the American Literary Translators Association that supported and encouraged this work's beginnings.

Thank you, Ben and Alan of The Song Cave, for seeing this book through to the end.

OTHER TITLES FROM THE SONG CAVE: